Phonetic Bible Stories

Daniel in the Lions' Den

M000036436

I BLESSED

Claudia Courtney ☆ Illustrated by Bill Clark

SAINT LOUIS

*For Anna, whose faith and friendship run
deep—Isaiah 40:31*

Note to Grown-ups

The love of reading is one of the greatest things you can instill in your child. It opens new horizons, exposes your child to new ideas, and provides information as well as entertainment.

This beginning reader series blends the best of two worlds— phonics to help your child learn to read and popular Bible stories to help your child learn to read God's Word. After you use a book in this series, open your child's Bible and read the story from God's Word. Emphasize to your child that this story is not make-believe—it's true, and we can believe every word in God's Holy Book.

Before you begin, review together the word, sound, and spelling list on page 16. Please note this Bible story is taken from Daniel 6. It emphasizes the short e sound, or phoneme, as in the words *best* and *blessed*. This story also contains two phrases with apostrophes—*lions' den* and *Daniel's God*. Review them with your early reader. Explain that their purpose is to show ownership (the den belonged to the lions, Daniel's God refers to the God Daniel chose to worship at a time when many others chose idols).

Your enthusiasm for reading, and especially for reading God's Word, should be contagious. Run your finger under each word as you read it, showing your child that it is the words that convey the actual story. Have your child join with you in reading repeated phrases.

Finally, have your child read the story as you offer plenty of praise. Pause to allow your youngster time to sound out words, but provide help when necessary to avoid frustration. When a mistake is made, invite your child to reread the sentence. This provides an appropriate opportunity to guide your early reader. Early success and your generous praise are keys to opening the door to your child's world of reading, especially to the joys of reading the Bible.

Claudia Courtney

Daniel did his job well. He
    was the best.
So the king set Daniel
    ahead of the rest.

Selfish men wanted to get
    Daniel.
They wanted a test so
    they would be best.

Men must pray only to the
    king, they pled, or be
    sent to the lions' den.
The king said yes.

4

Three times every day, Daniel still bent to
  pray. He kept God first.

The clever men saw Daniel bent to pray.
They went to tell the king.
They went to arrest Daniel.

The men were now content.
Daniel would be fed to the lions and
the king would like them best.

The king felt pressed, yet he held to
   the test.
He sent his friend Daniel to the lions.
But first, the king said to Daniel,
   "May your God rescue you from
      death."

Daniel fell over the edge to the center of the den.
Daniel bent to pray, and the lions stepped away.
God sent His angel to protect!

Daniel slept. The lions slept.
Yet the king had no rest.

10

The next day, the king sped to the den to check on his friend.
Daniel was safe! God protects!

Daniel was let out of the lions' den.
He blessed God and the king.

The king sent the rebels to the
   lions' den.
They met their end instead of
   Daniel.

Now the king was content, and
   he professed,
"God saves! God protects!
Daniel's God is best!"

Word Lists

phoneme *e*	friend	set
angel	get	slept
arrest	held	sped
bent	kept	stepped
best	let	tell
blessed	men	test
center	met	them
check	next	wanted
clever	pled	well
content	professed	went
den	protect	yes
edge	pressed	yet
end	rebels	phoneme *ea*
every	rescue	ahead
fed	rest	death
fell	selfish	instead
felt	sent	

Other Words

a	he	on	their
and	his	only	they
away	is	or	three
be	job	out	times
but	king	over	to
Daniel	like	pray	was
Daniel's	lions	safe	were
day	lions'	said	would
did	may	saves	you
first	must	saw	your
from	no	so	
God	now	still	
had	of	the	

16